Living or Nonliving?

Nathan Mills

Rosen Readers

Rosen Classroom™

New York

Published in 2013 by The Rosen Publishing Group, Inc.
29 East 21st Street, New York, NY 10010

Book Design: Katelyn Londino

Photo Credits: Cover malcolm park/Garden Picture Library/Getty Images; p. 4 © iStockphoto.com/viki2win; p. 5 CandyBox Images/Shutterstock.com; p. 6 Juan Jose Rodriguez Velandia/Shutterstock.com; pp. 7, 15 (boy with book) wavebreakmedia ltd/Shutterstock.com; pp. 8, 15 (dog with ball) Stephen Bures/Shutterstock.com; pp. 9, 15 (flower on table) Stefanie Mohr Photography/Shutterstock.com; pp. 10, 15, 16 (butterfly) Don Farrall/Photodisc/Getty Images; pp. 11, 15, 16 (chair in grass) V. J. Matthew/Shutterstock.com; pp. 12, 15, 16 (kitten with bowl) Magone/Shutterstock.com; pp. 13, 15 (girl with shoe) Image Source/Image Source/Getty Images; p. 14 © iStockphoto.com/mediaphotos.

ISBN: 978-1-4488-8746-0
6-pack ISBN: 978-1-4488-8747-7

Manufactured in the United States of America

CPSIA Compliance Information: Batch #WS12RC: For further information contact Rosen Publishing, New York, New York at 1-800-237-9932.

Word Count: 125

Contents

What is a living thing?
What is a nonliving thing?

Living things need food and water to live.

Nonliving things are not alive.
They don't need food and water.

A boy is a living thing.
A book is a nonliving thing.

A dog is a living thing.
A ball is a nonliving thing.

A flower is a living thing.
A table is a nonliving thing.

A butterfly is a living thing.
A jar is a nonliving thing.

Grass is a living thing.
A chair is a nonliving thing.

A kitten is a living thing.
A dish is a nonliving thing.

A girl is a living thing.
A shoe is a nonliving thing.

Can you name other living things?
Can you name other nonliving things, too?

Living or Nonliving?

living

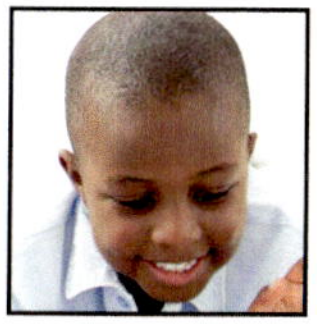
boy

dog

flower

butterfly

grass

kitten

girl

nonliving

book

ball

table

jar

chair

dish

shoe

Words to Know

butterfly

chair

dish

Index